WEDDING FAVORITES
FOR ORGAN

T0101617

ISBN 978-1-4803-4209-5

SHAWNEE PRESS

Exclusively Distributed By

HAL•LEONARD®
CORPORATION
7777 W. BLUEMOUND RD. P.O. BOX 13819 MILWAUKEE, WI 53213

Visit Hal Leonard Online at
www.halleonard.com

Visit Shawnee Press Online at
www.shawneepress.com

Can't Help Falling in Love

Electronic Organs

Upper: String (or Violin) 8'
Lower: Flute 8', Diapason 8'
Pedal: 16', 8' Sustain
Vib./Trem.. On, Full

Drawbar Organs

Upper: 00 5855 555
Lower: (00) 6534 211
Pedal: 53 Sustain
Vib./Trem.: On, Full

Words and Music by GEORGE DAVID WEISS,
HUGO PERETTI and LUIGI CREATORE

Could I Have This Dance

Electronic Organs
Upper: Flutes (or Tibias) 8', 4', String 8'
Lower: Flutes 8', 4', String 8'
Pedal: 8', Sustain
Vib./Trem.: On, Fast

Drawbar Organs
Upper: 80 0800 000
Lower: (00) 7400 000
Pedal: String Bass
Vib./Trem.: On, Fast

Words and Music by WAYLAND HOLYFIELD
and BOB HOUSE

Gabriel's Oboe

from the Motion Picture THE MISSION

Upper: *mp*
Lower: *p*
Pedal: *p*

Words and Music by
ENNIO MORRICONE

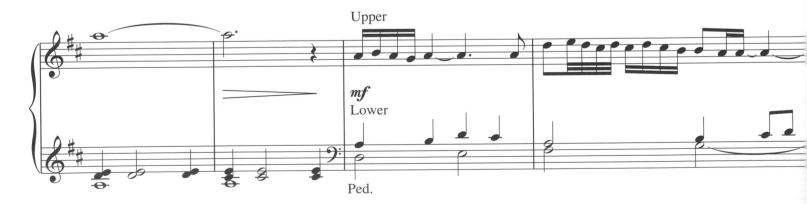

Lower
cresc.
No Ped.

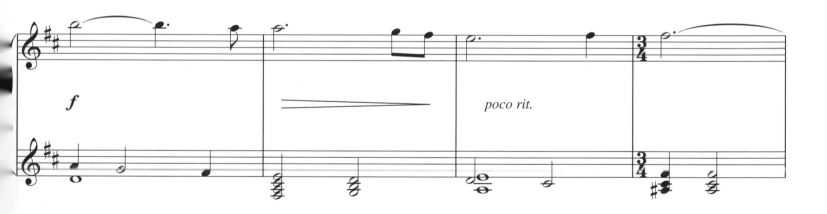

f

poco rit.

Ped.

Grow Old with Me

Electronic Organs

Upper: Flutes (or Tibias) 16', 4', String 8'
Lower: Melodia 8', Piano
Pedal: 16', 8'
Vib./Trem.: On, Fast

Drawbar Organs

Upper: 60 3616 113
Lower: (00) 7634 211
Pedal: 25
Vib./Trem.: On, Fast

Words and Music by
JOHN LENNON

Bless the Broken Road

Upper: *mf*
Lower: *mp*
Pedal: *mp*

Words and Music by MARCUS HUMMON,
BOBBY BOYD and JEFF HANNA

Moderately slow

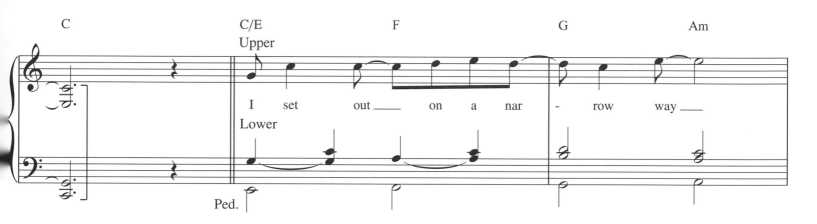

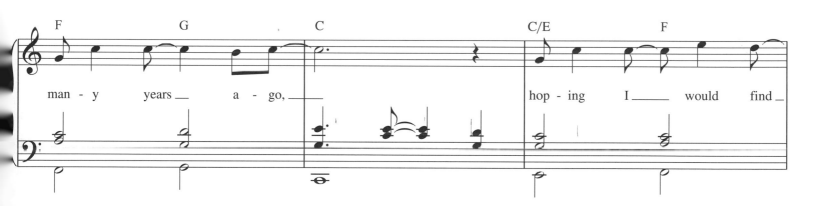

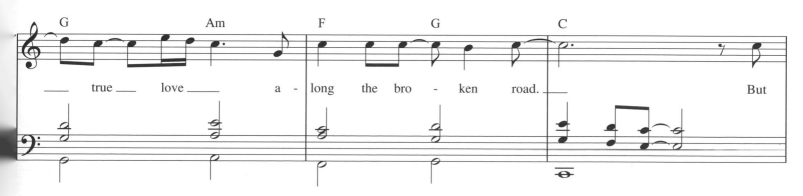

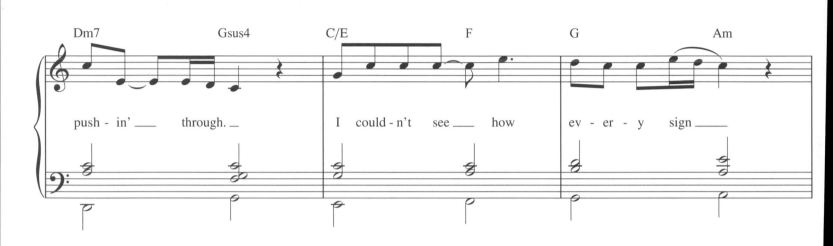

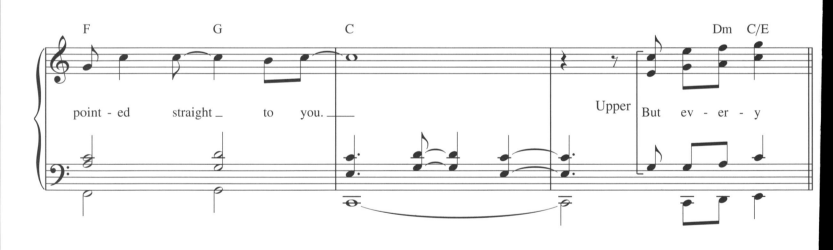

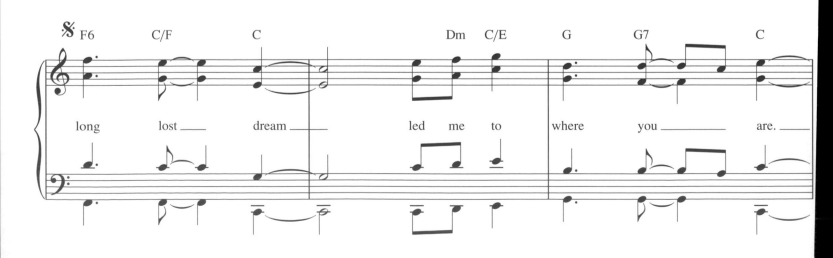

To Coda

God blessed __ the bro - ken __ road that led me straight __ to you. __
Lower

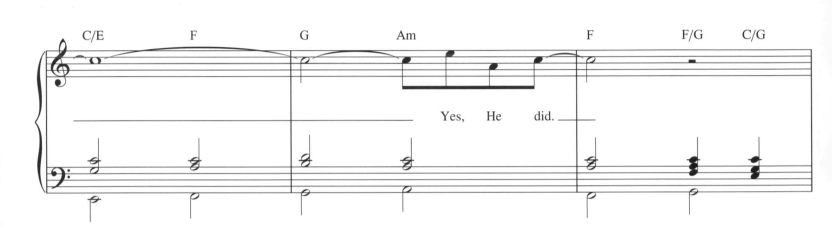

Yes, He did. __

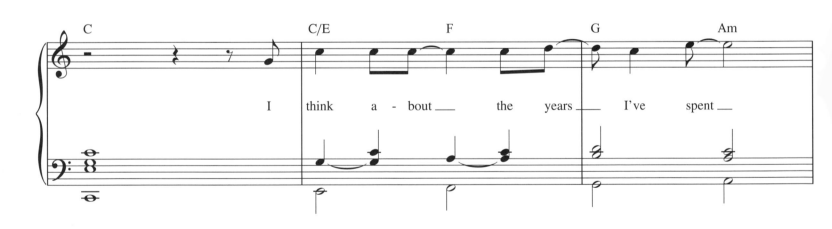

I think a - bout __ the years __ I've spent __

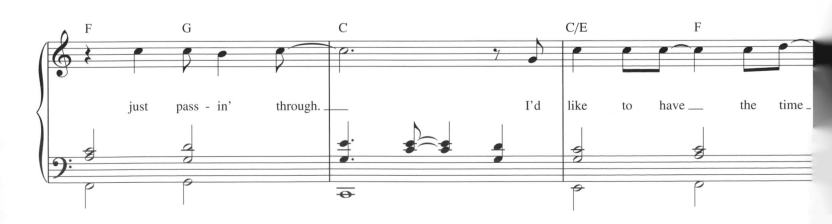

just pass - in' through. __ I'd like to have __ the time __

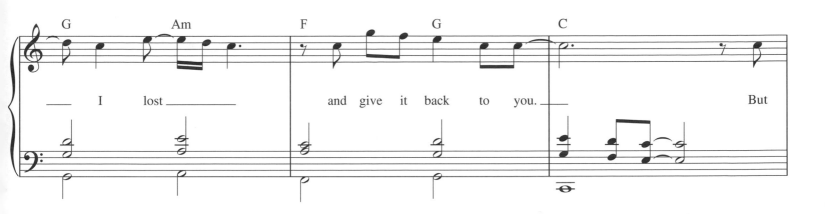

I lost _____ and give it back to you. _____ But

you just smile __ and take __ my hand. __ You've been there, __ you

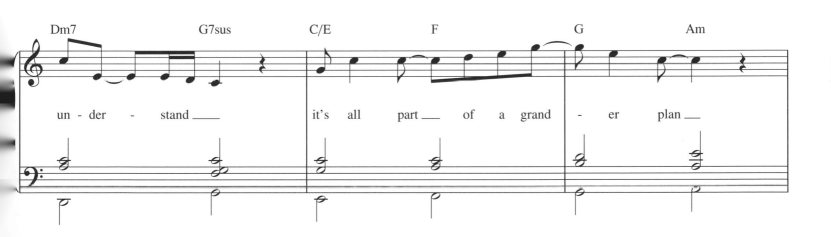

un - der - stand _____ it's all part __ of a grand - er plan __

D.S. al Coda

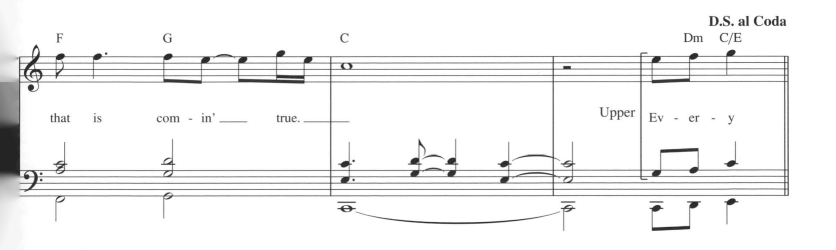

that is com - in' _____ true. _____ Upper Ev - er - y

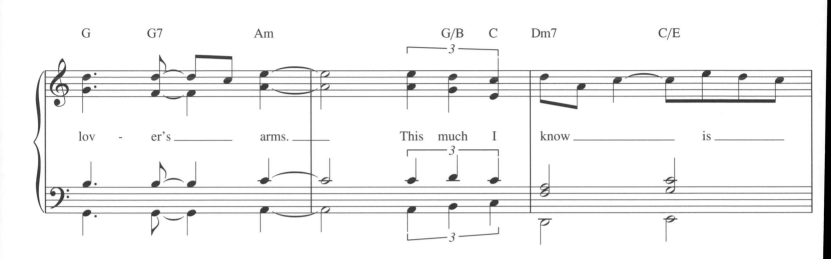

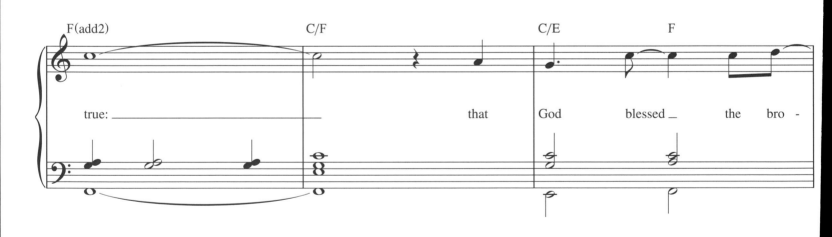

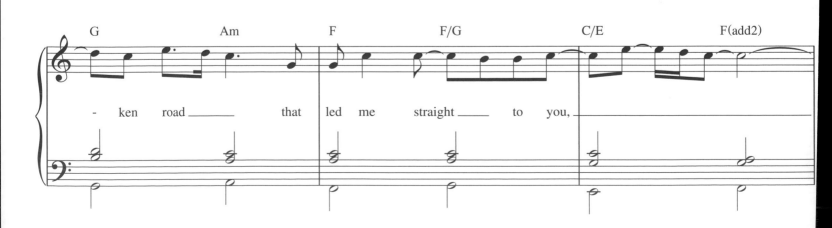

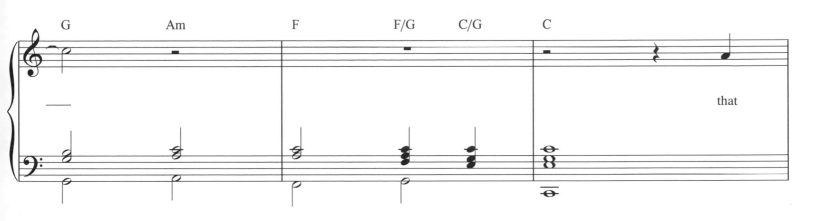

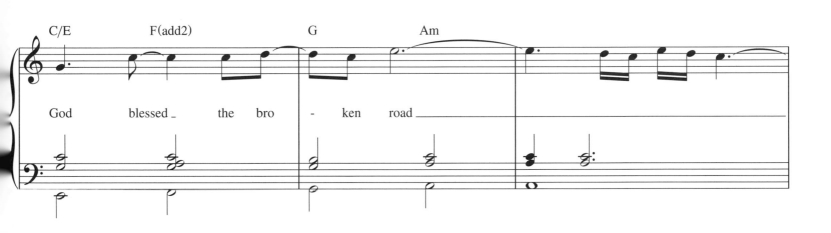

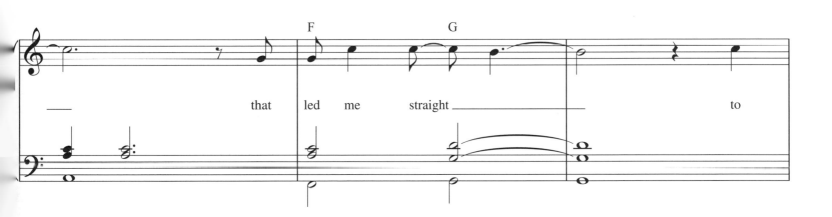

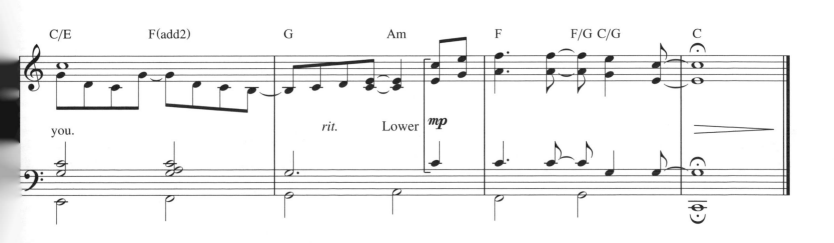

The Hawaiian Wedding Song
(Ke Kali Nei Au)

Electronic Organs
Upper: Hawaiian Guitar Preset
Lower: Flutes 8′, 4′, String 8′
Pedal: String Bass
Vib./Trem.: Vibrato On
Automatic Rhythm: Fox Trot

Drawbar Organs
Upper: Hawaiian Guitar Preset
Lower: (00) 4533 210
Pedal: 43
Vib./Trem.: Vibrato On
Automatic Rhythm: Fox Trot

English Lyrics by AL HOFFMAN and DICK MANNING
Hawaiian Lyrics and Music by CHARLES E. KING

Highland Cathedral

Upper: *ff*
Lower: *f*
Pedal: *f*

By MICHAEL KORB
and ULRICH ROEVER

Stately March, in two

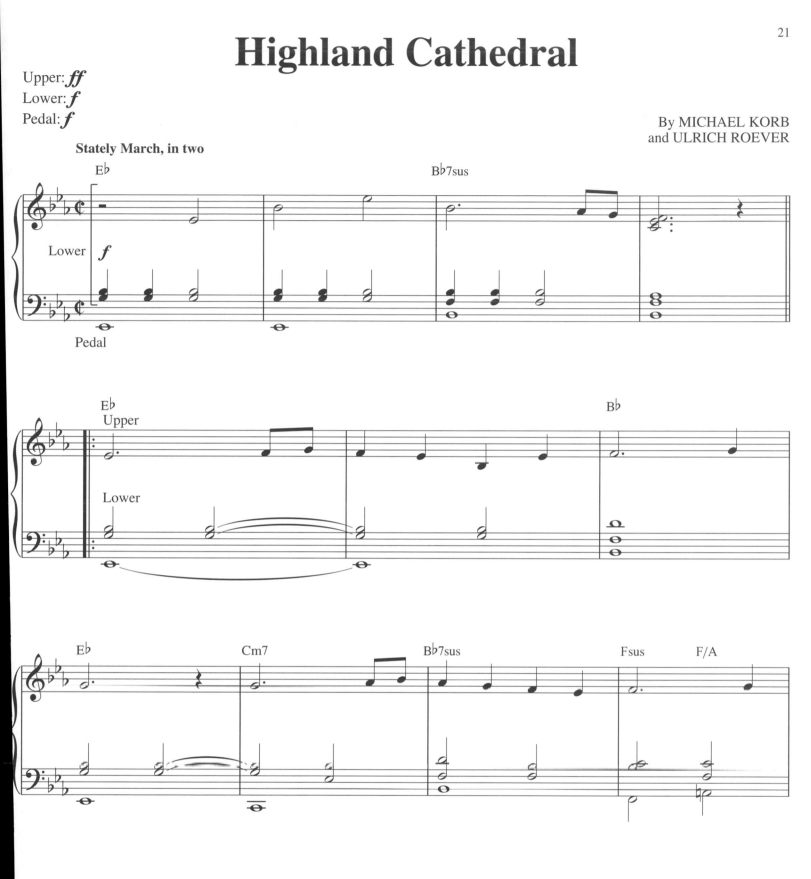

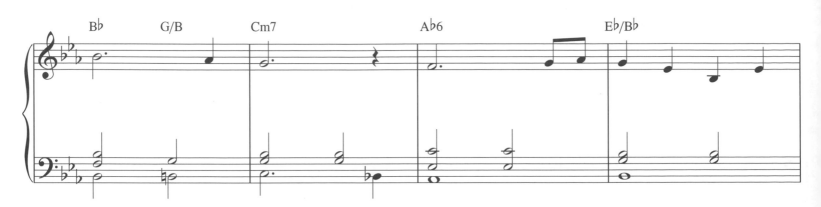

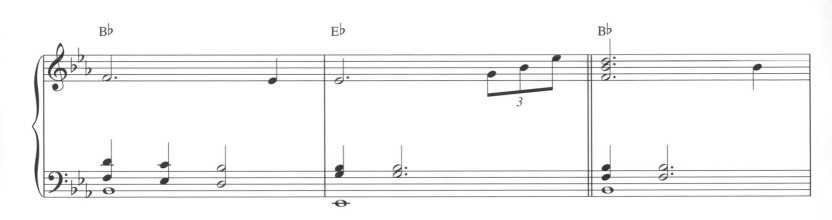

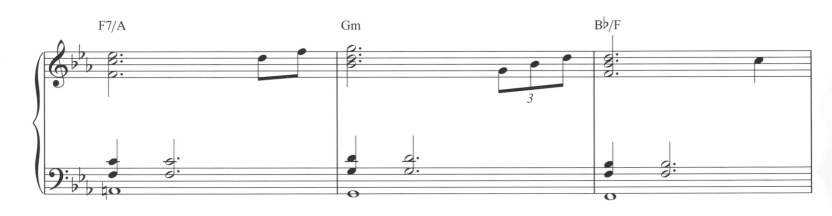

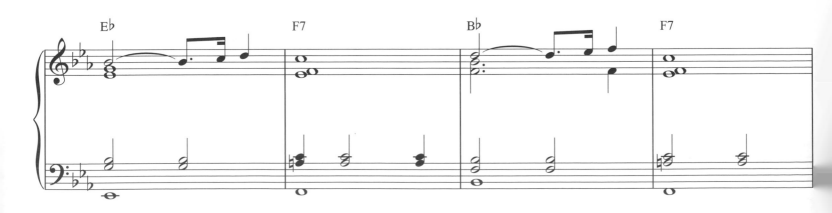

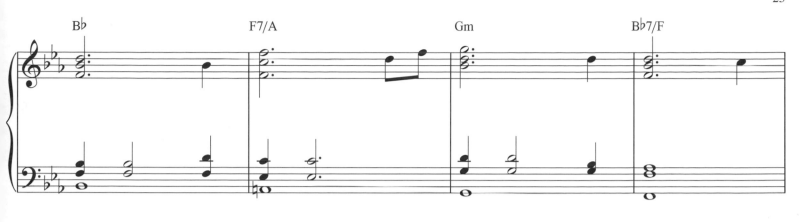

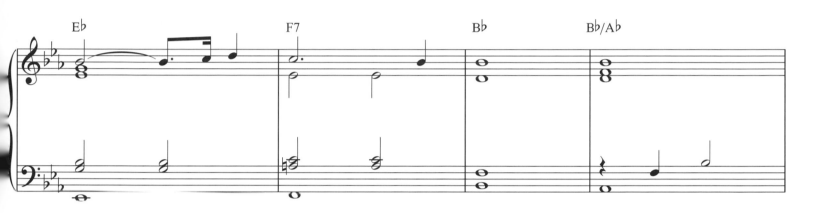

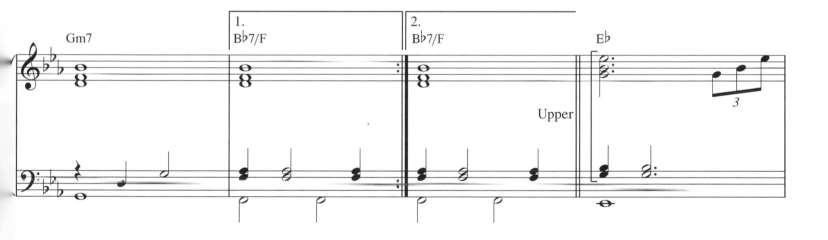

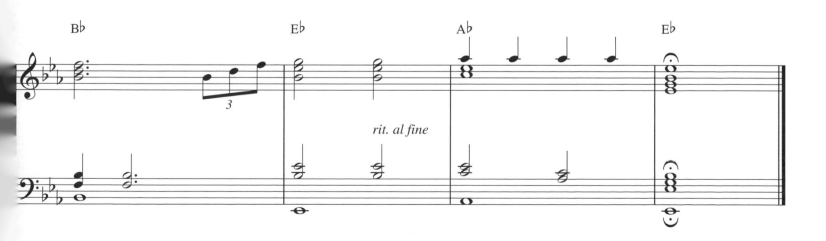

Household of Faith

Electronic Organs
Upper: Clarinet 8'
Lower: Melodia, String 4'
Pedal: 16', 8'
Vib./Trem: On, Fast

Drawbar Organs
Upper: 80 8104 103
Lower: (00)
Pedal: 34
Vib./Trem: On, Fast

Words by BRENT LAMB
Music by JOHN ROSASCO

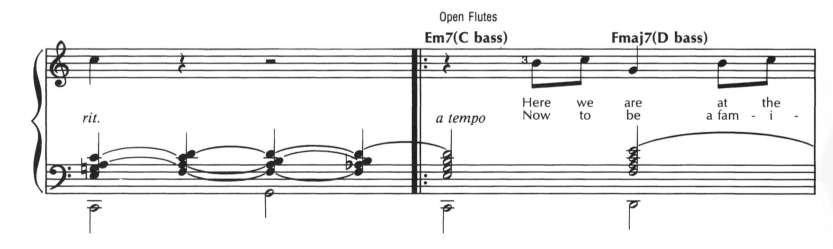

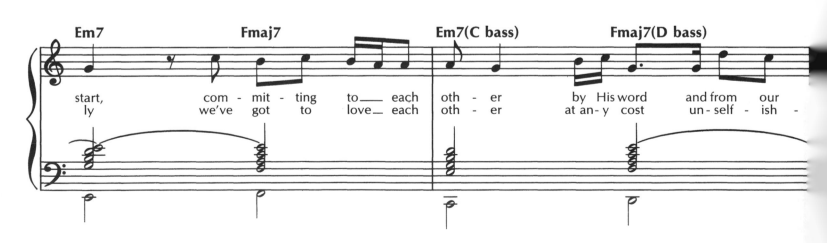

I Love You
from MEXICAN HAYRIDE

Electronic Organs
Upper: Flutes (or Tibias) 16′, 5⅓′, 2′
Lower: Flute 8′, String 4′
Pedal: 8′, Sustain
Vib./Trem.: Off

Tonebar Organs
Upper: 87 0008 000
Lower: (00) 6540 050
Pedal: 44 String Bass
Vib./Trem.: Off

Words and Music by
COLE PORTER

How Deep Is Your Love

Electronic Organs
Upper: Flutes (or Tibias) 16′, 8′, 5⅓′, 4′
Lower: Flutes 8′, 4′
Pedal: String Bass
Vib./Trem.: On, Slow

Drawbar Organs
Upper: 80 8505 103
Lower: (00) 8303 004
Pedal: String Bass
Vib./Trem.: On, Slow

Words and Music by BARRY GIBB,
ROBIN GIBB and MAURICE GIBB

I Want You, I Need You, I Love You

Electronic Organs

Upper: Flute (or Tibia) 16',
       Clarinet 8'
Lower: Flutes 8', 4', String 4'
Pedal: 16', 8' Sustain
Vib./Trem.: On Full

Moderately Slow

Drawbar Organs

Upper: 60 8080 806
Lower: (00) 7654 321
Pedal: 55 Sustain
Vib./Trem.: On, Full

Words and Music by MAURICE MYSELS
and IRA KOSLOFF

I Will Be Here

Upper: *mf*
Lower: *mp*
Pedal: *mp*

Words and Music by
STEVEN CURTIS CHAPMAN

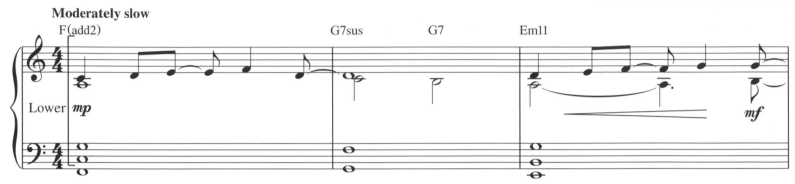

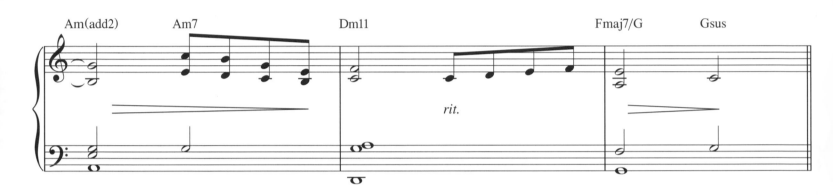

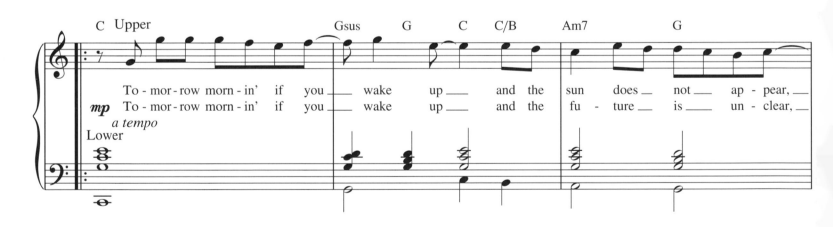

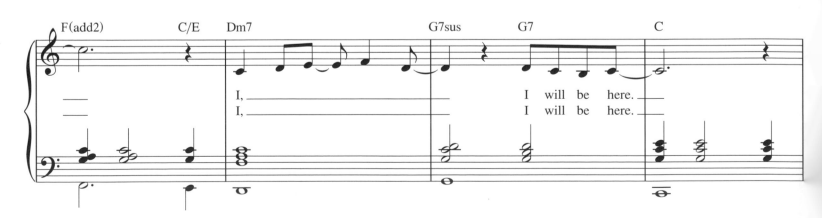

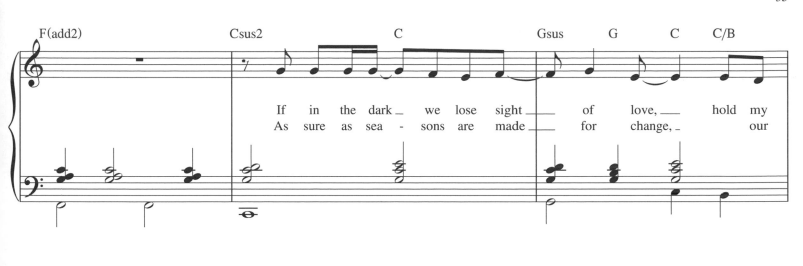

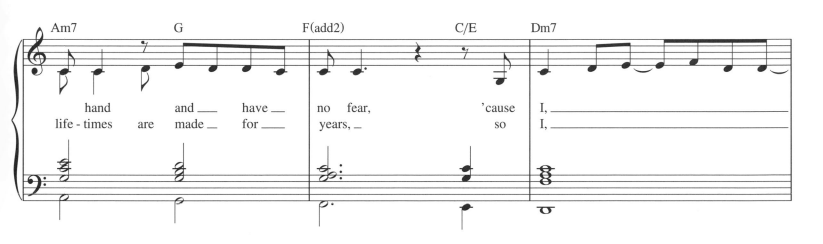

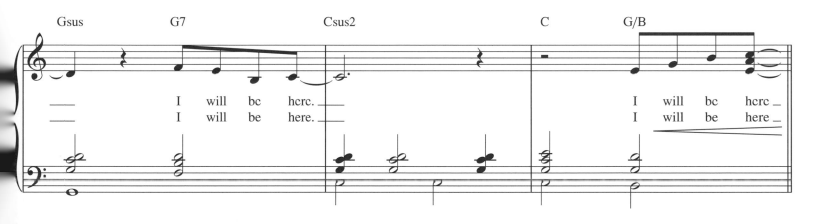

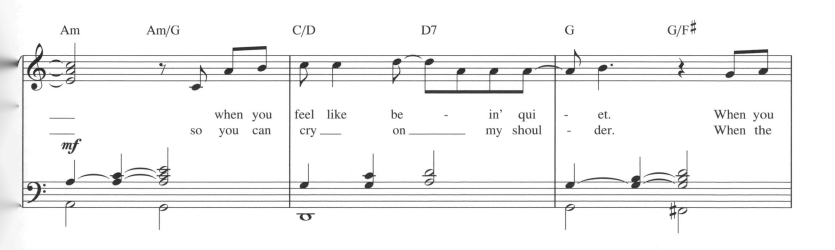

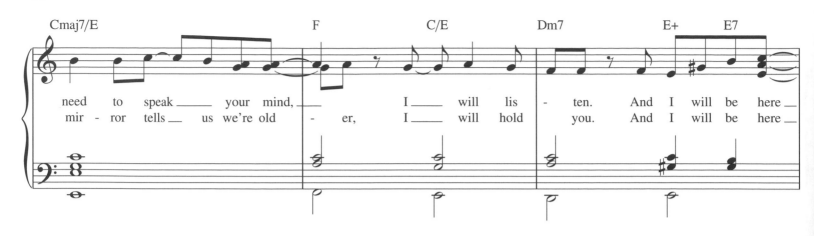

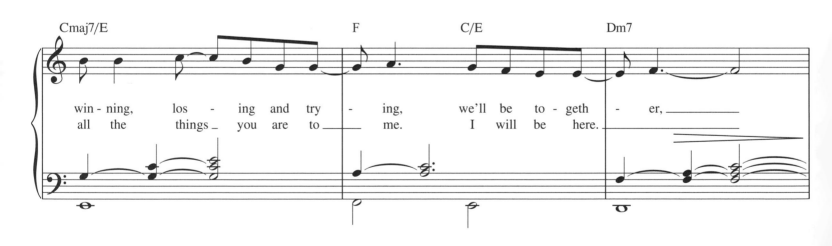

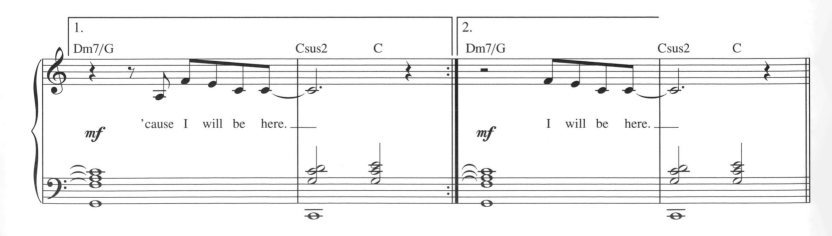

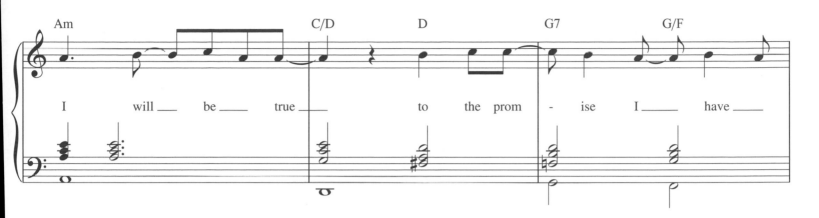

I will _ be _ true _ to the prom - ise I _ have _

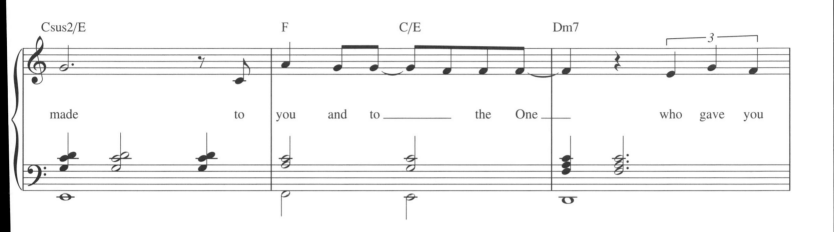

made to you and to _ the One _ who gave you

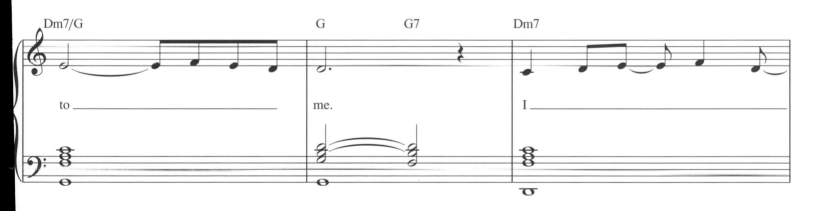

to _ me. I _

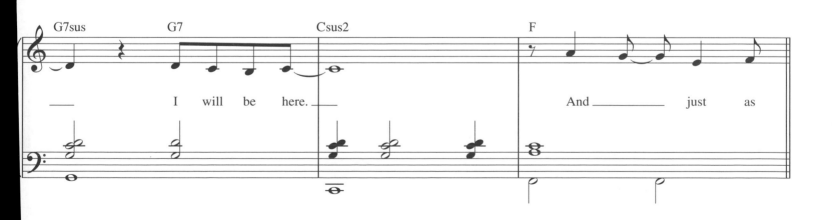

_ I will be here. _ And _ just as

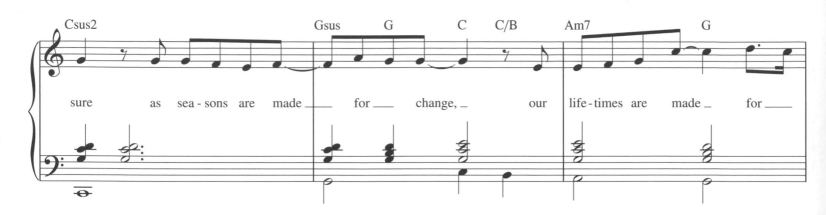

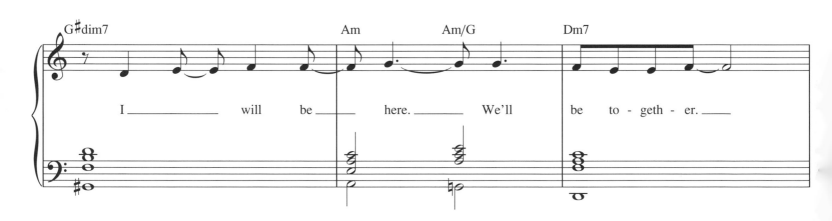

If We Only Have Love
(Quand on n'a que l'amour)
from JACQUES BREL IS ALIVE AND WELL AND LIVING IN PARIS

Electronic Organs
Upper: Flutes (or Tibias) 16′, 8′, 2′,
       Trumpet
Lower: Flute 4′, Diapason 8′
Pedal: String Bass
Vib./Trem.: On, Fast

Drawbar Organs
Upper: 80 6368 006
Lower: (00) 8365 002
Pedal: String Bass
Vib./Trem.: On, Fast

French Words and Music by JACQUES BREL
English Words by MORT SHUMAN and ERIC BLAU

Thoughtfully

Lyrics:
If we on-ly have love / If we on-ly have love
then to-mor-row will dawn; / we can reach those in pain.
And the days of our years / We can heal all our wounds
will rise on that morn / we can use our own names
If we on-ly have love, / If we on-ly have love,
to em-brace with-out fears / we can melt all the guns

Just the Way You Are

Electronic Organs
Upper: Flutes (or Tibias) 16′, 8′, 5⅓′, 4′, 2′
Lower: Flutes 8′, 4′, Diapason 8′,
      Reed 8′
Pedal: 16′, 8′
Vib./Trem.: On, Fast

Tonebar Organs
Upper: 86 6606 000
Lower: (00) 7732 211
Pedal: 55
Vib./Trem.: On, Fast

Words and Music by
BILLY JOEL

Sunrise, Sunset

from the Musical FIDDLER ON THE ROOF

Electronic Organs
Upper: Flute (or Tibia) 4', Oboe 8'
Lower: Flute 8', String 8'
Pedal: 8'
Vib./Trem.: On, Fast

Drawbar Organs
Upper: 00 6640 000
Lower: (00) 5323 001
Pedal: 34
Vib./Trem.: On, Fast

Words by SHELDON HARNICK
Music by JERRY BOCK

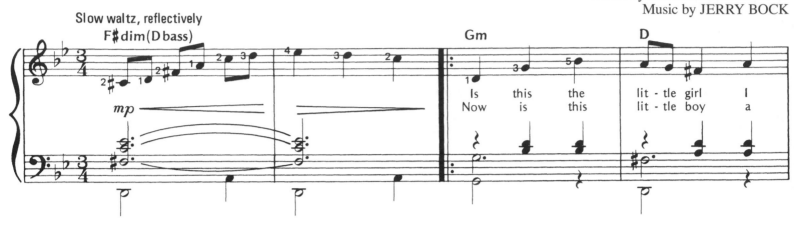

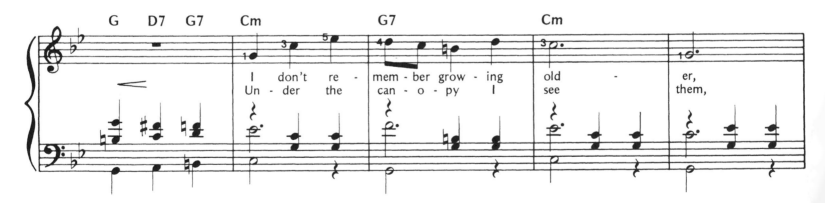

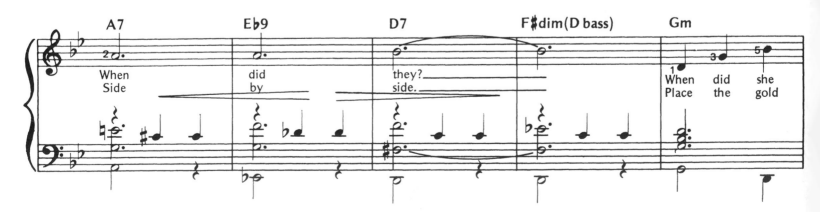

The Lord's Prayer

Electronic Organs
Upper: Strings 8', 4'
Lower: Diapason 8', Melodia (opt.)
Pedal: 16', 8'
Vib./Trem.: On, Slow

Drawbar Organs
Upper: 80 7105 103
Lower: (00) 7303 002
Pedal: 45
Vib./Trem.: On, Slow

By ALBERT H. MALOTTE

Slowly, in a religious manner

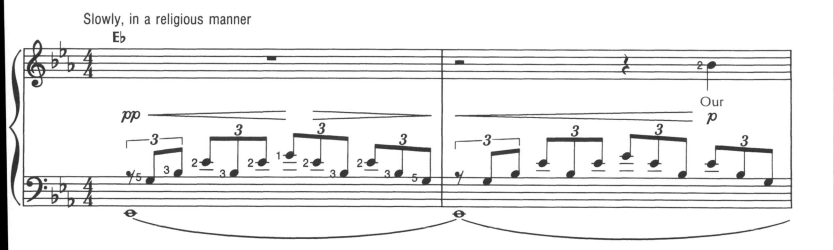

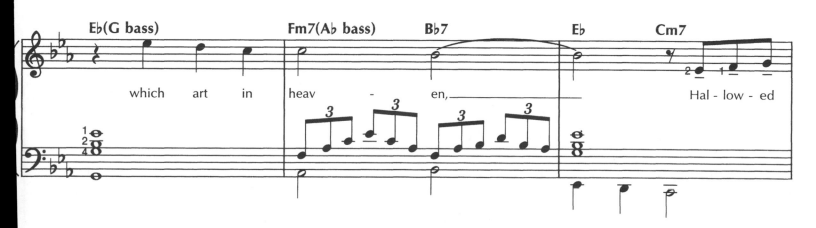

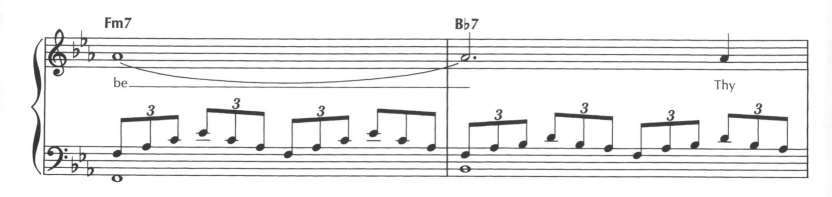

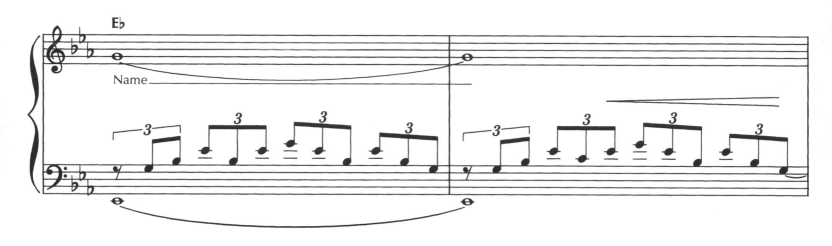

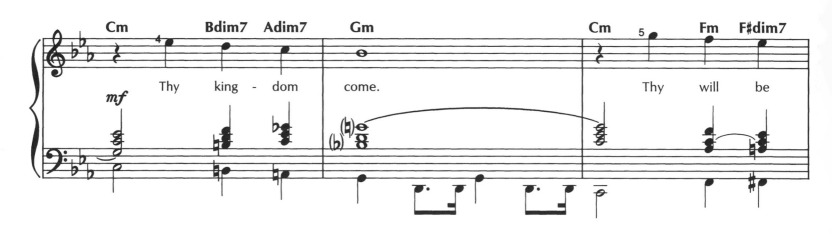

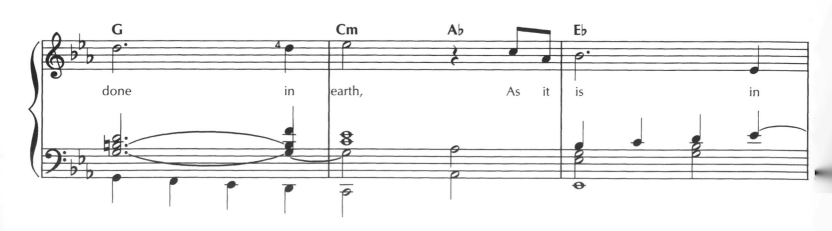

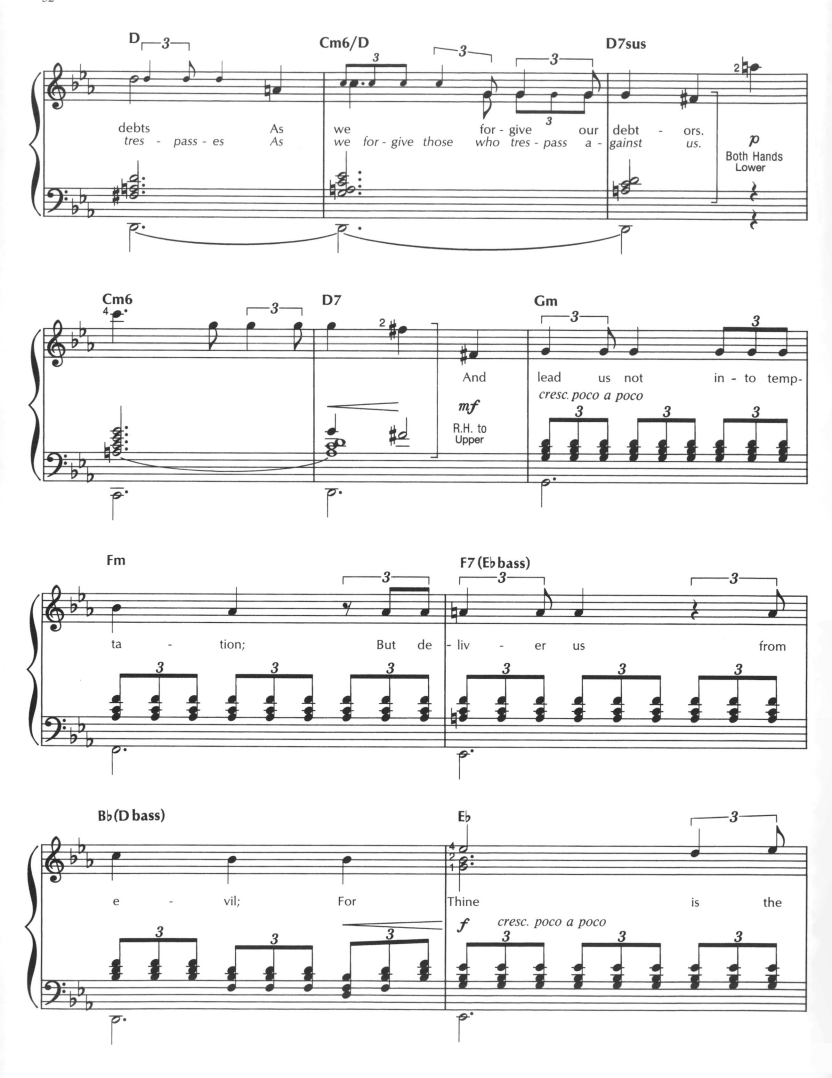

Till the End of Time

from TILL THE END OF TIME

(Based on Chopin's Polonaise)

Electronic Organs
Upper: Piano
Lower: Flute 8', 4'
Pedal: 16', 8'
Vib./Trem: On, Fast

Drawbar Organs
Upper: Preset Piano or 80 6606 000
Lower: (00) 7400 000
Pedal: 34
Vib./Trem: On, Fast

Words and Music by BUDDY KAYE
and TED MOSSMAN

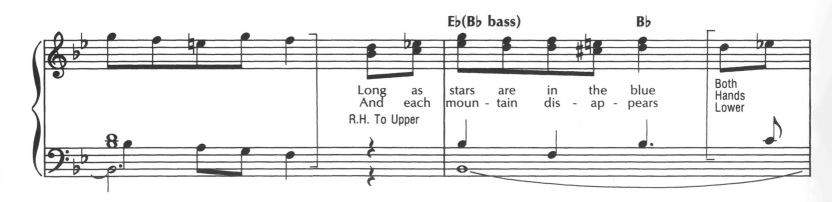

True Love

from HIGH SOCIETY

Electronic Organs
Upper: Flutes (or Tibias) 16', 4', String 8'
Lower: Flutes 8', 4', Diapason 8'
Pedal: String Bass
Vib./Trem.. On, Fast

Drawbar Organs
Upper: 60 3616 113
Lower: (00) 7634 212
Pedal: String Bass
Vib./Trem.: On, Fast

Words and Music by
COLE PORTER

58

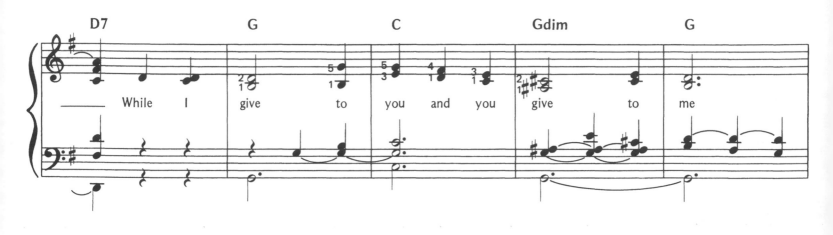

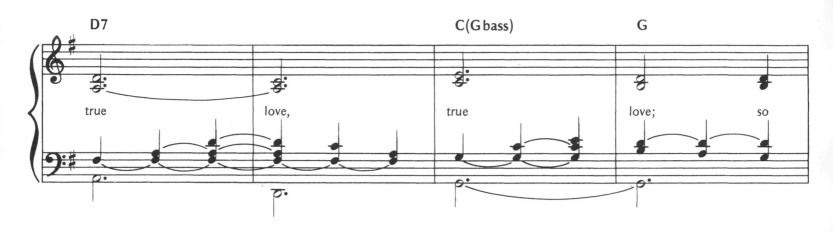

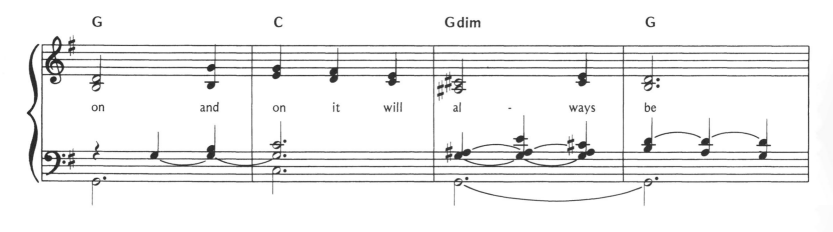

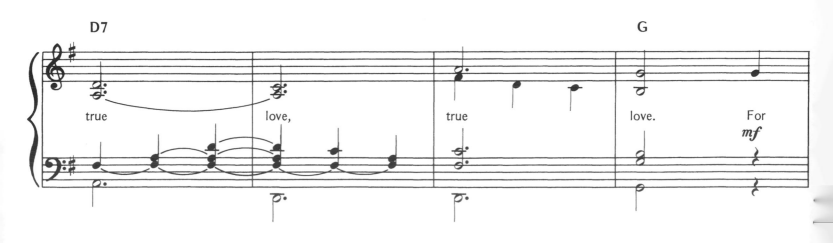

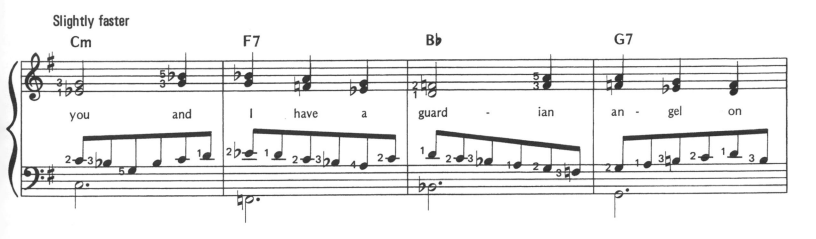

you and I have a guard - ian an - gel on

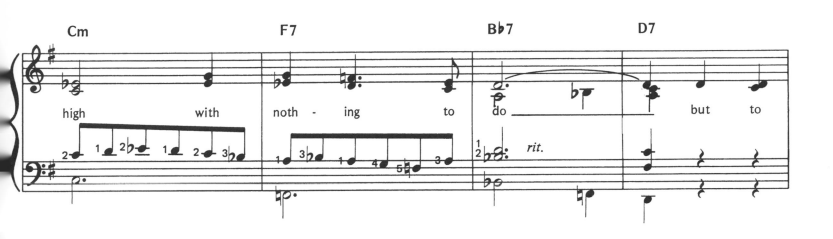

high with noth - ing to do but to

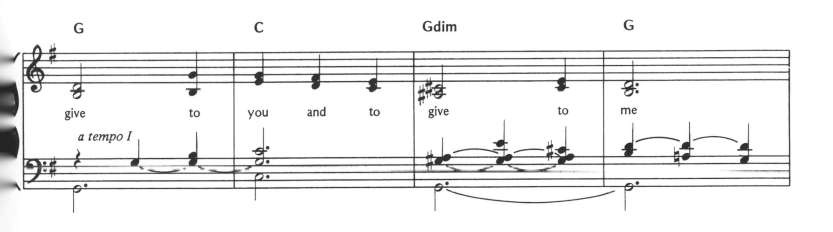

give to you and to give to me

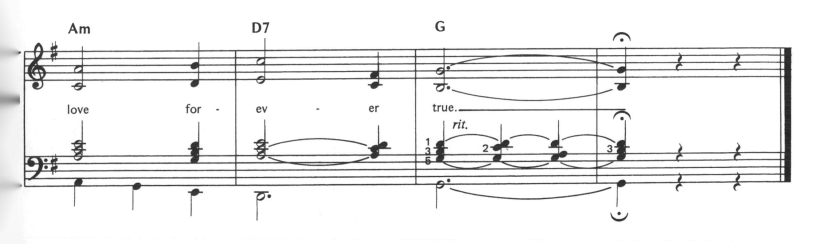

love for - ev - er true.

We've Only Just Begun

Upper: *mf*
Lower: *mp*
Pedal: *mp*

Words and Music by ROGER NICHOLS
and PAUL WILLIAMS

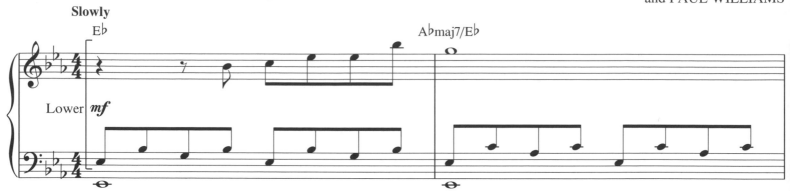

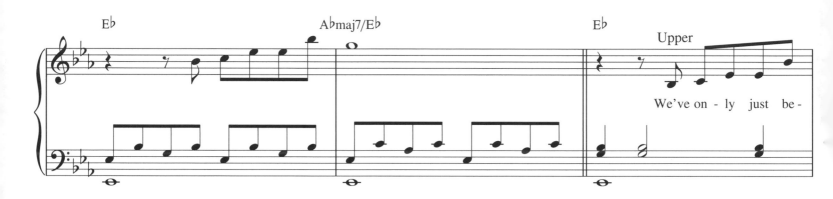

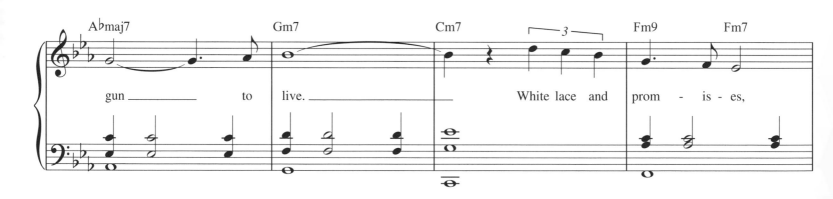

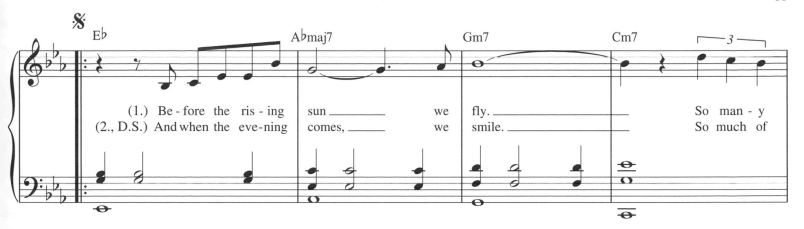

(1.) Be - fore the ris - ing sun _____ we fly. _____ So man - y
(2., D.S.) And when the eve-ning comes, _____ we smile. _____ So much of

To Coda ⊕

roads to choose, we start out walk - ing and learn to run. _____
life a - head, we'll find a place _ where there's room to grow. _____

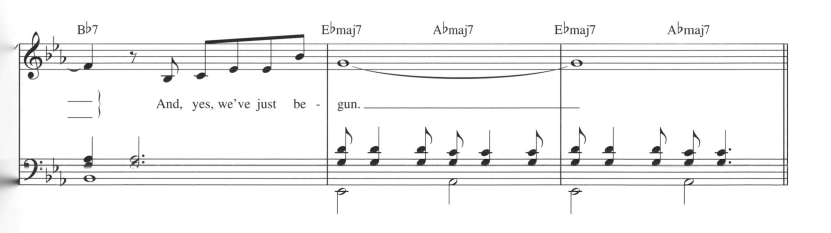

And, yes, we've just be - gun. _____

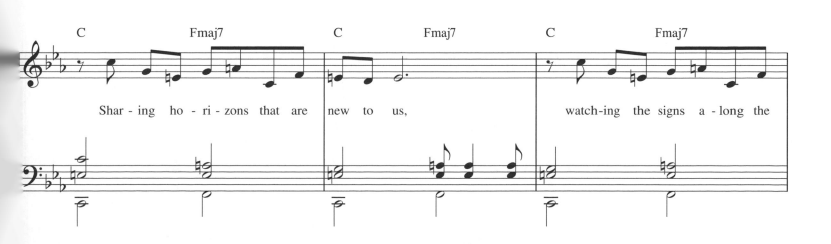

Shar - ing ho - ri - zons that are new to us, watch-ing the signs a - long the

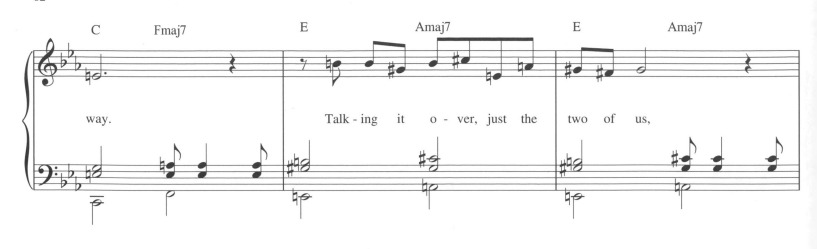

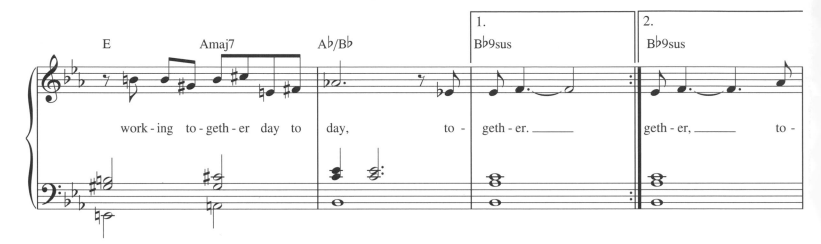

Wedding Song
(There Is Love)

Upper: *mp*
Lower: *p*
Pedal: *p*

Words and Music by
PAUL STOOKEY

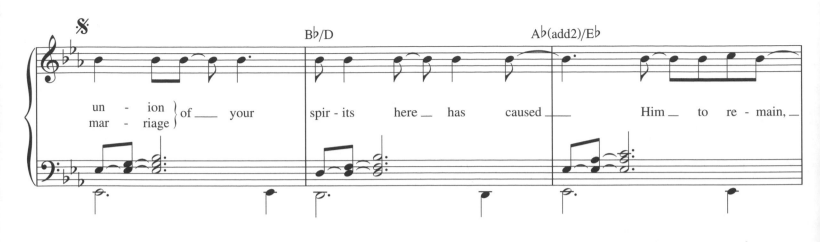

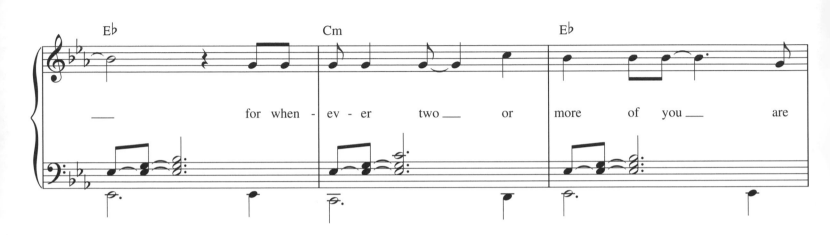

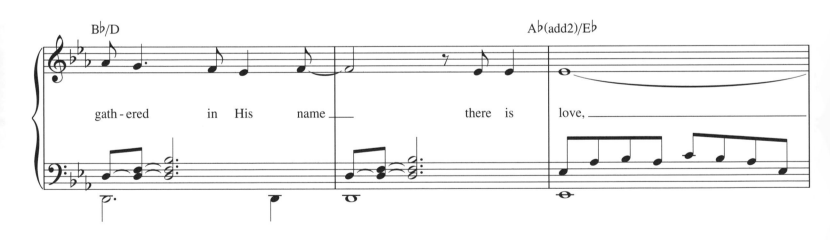

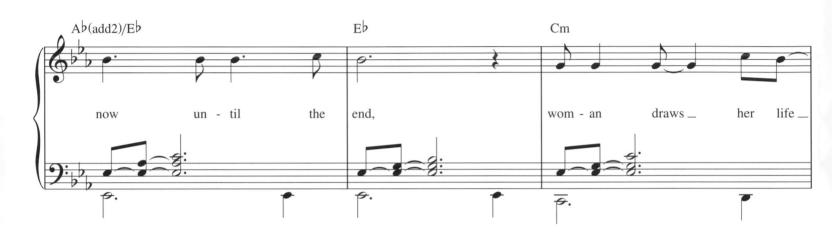

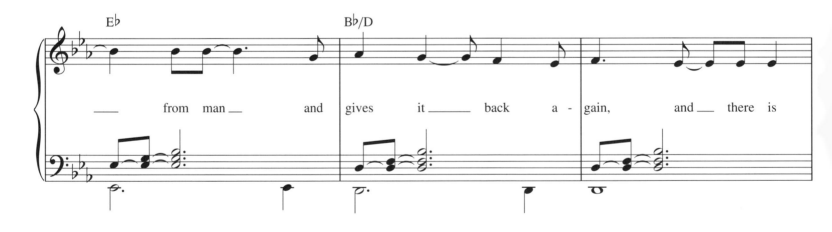

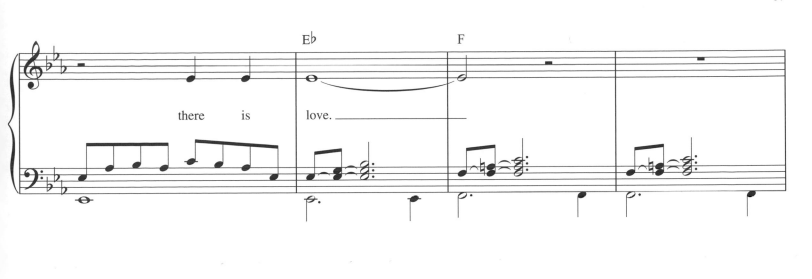

there is love.

Well then, what's to be the rea-

-son for be-com-ing man and wife? Is it

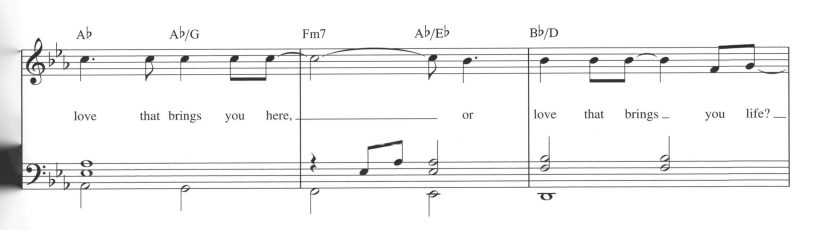

love that brings you here, or love that brings you life?

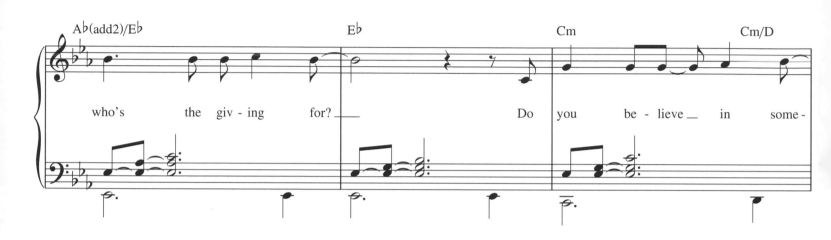

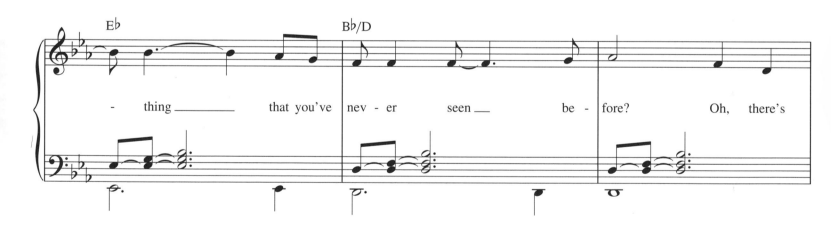

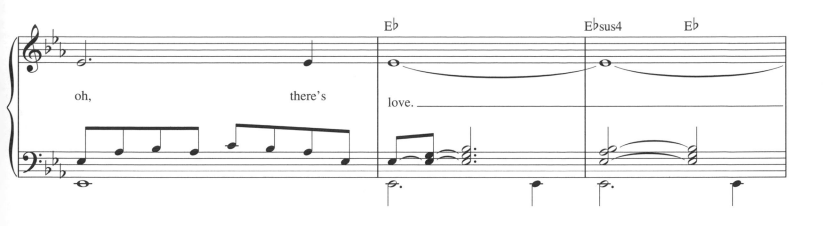

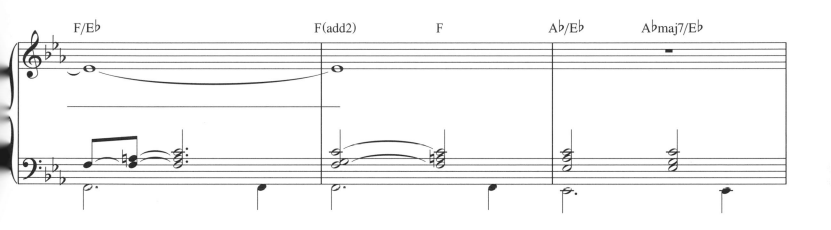

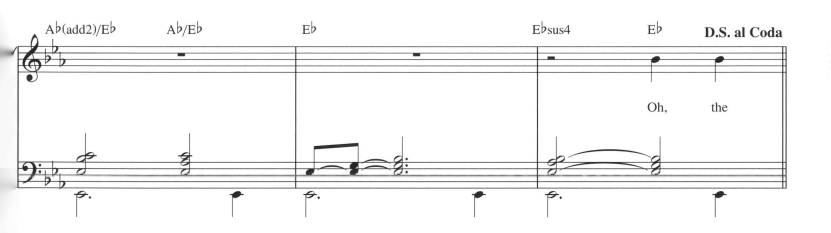

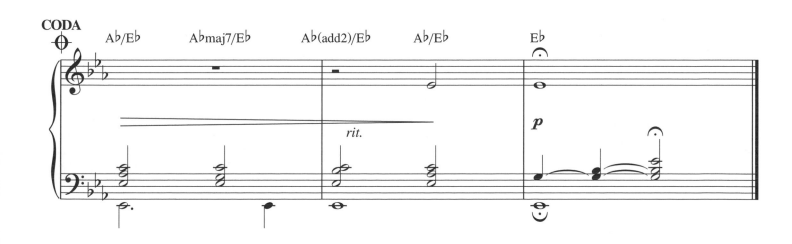

Wedding Processional

from THE SOUND OF MUSIC

Electronic Organs

Upper: Flutes (or Tibias) 16′, 8′, 4′, 2′,
      Strings 8′, 4′, Trumpet
Lower: Flutes 8′, 4′, Strings 8′, 4′,
      Reed 8′
Pedal: 16′, 8′
Vib./Trem.: Off

Drawbar Organs

Upper: 80 7104 001
Lower: (00) 8512 002
Pedal: 65
Vib./Trem.: Off

Lyrics by OSCAR HAMMERSTEIN II
Music by RICHARD RODGERS

Stately march

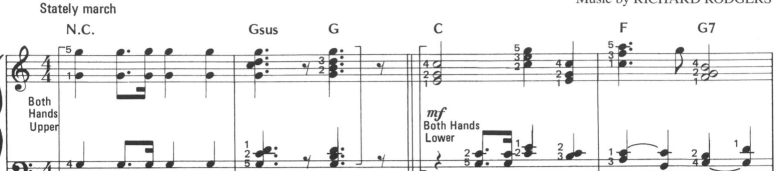

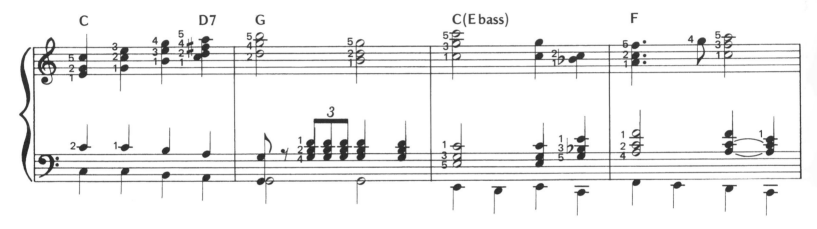

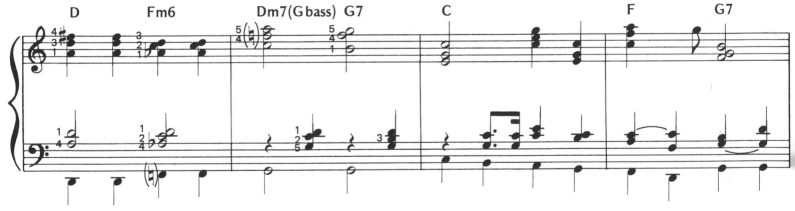

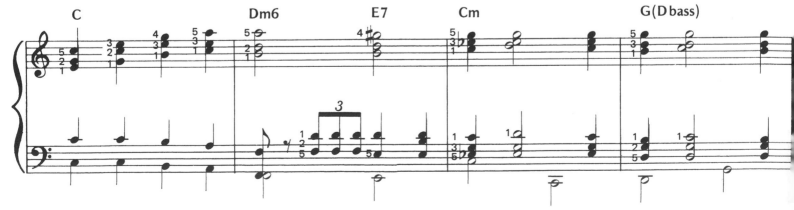

When You Say Nothing at All

Upper: *mf*
Lower: *mp*
Pedal: *mp*

Words and Music by DON SCHLITZ
and PAUL OVERSTREET

Moderately slow

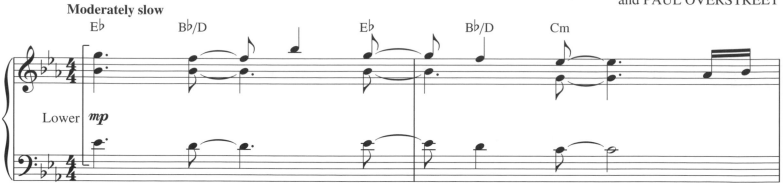

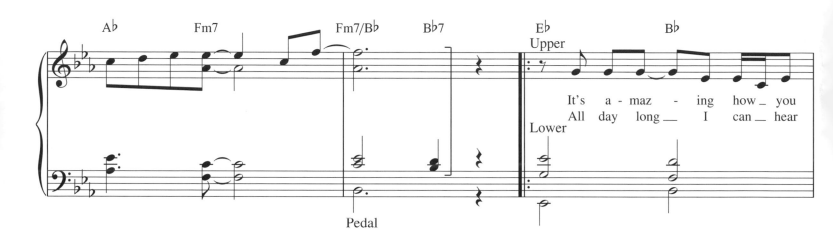

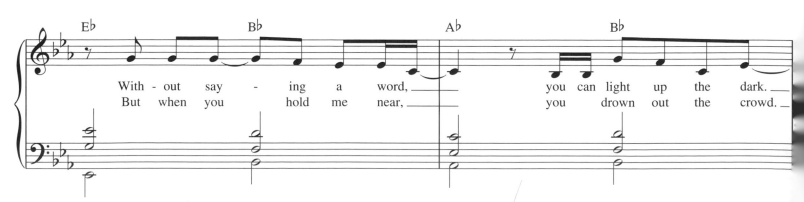

Eb   Bb   Ab   Bb

touch   of   your   hand ___ says   you'll   catch ___ me   if   ev –   er   I   fall.

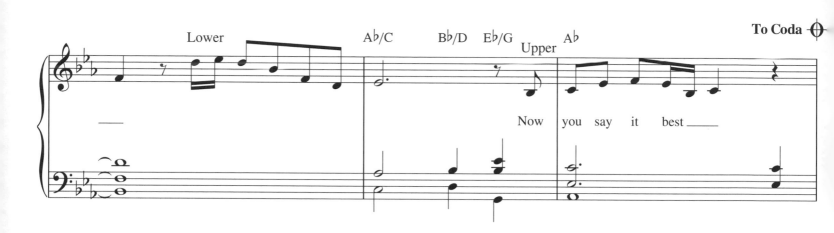

To Coda ⊕

Lower   Ab/C   Bb/D   Eb/G   Ab

Upper

___   Now   you   say   it   best ___

1.

Bb   Eb

when   you   say   noth –   ing   at   all. ___

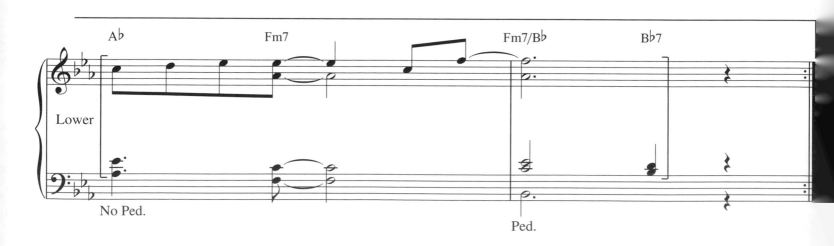

Ab   Fm7   Fm7/Bb   Bb7

Lower

No Ped.   Ped.

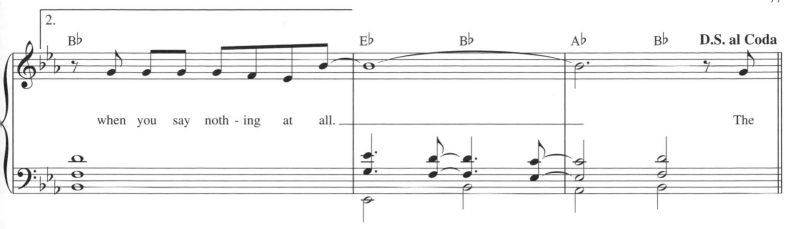

when you say noth-ing at all. _____ The

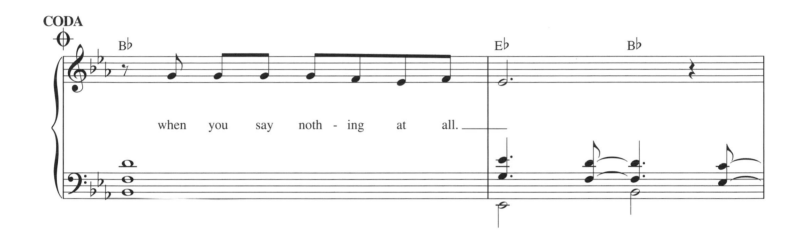

when you say noth-ing at all. _____

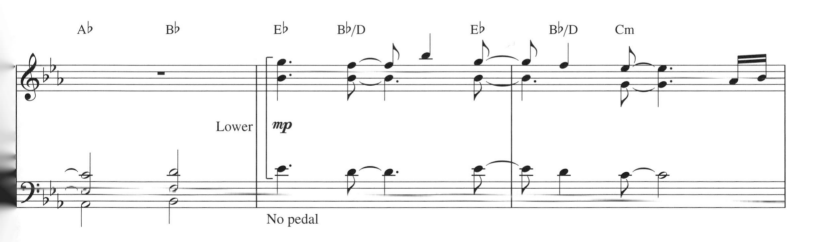

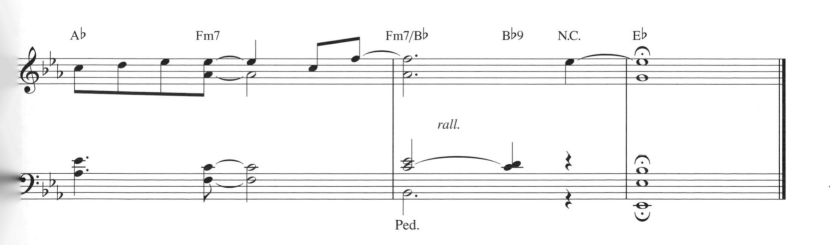

When I Need You

Electronic Organs
Upper: Flutes (or Tibias) 16', 4', 2'
Lower: Flutes 8', 4'
Pedal: 8'
Vib./Trem.: On, Fast

Drawbar Organs
Upper: 30 5202 002
Lower: (00) 6002 001
Pedal: 04
Vib./Trem.: On, Fast

Words and Music by CAROLE BAYER SAGER
and ALBERT HAMMOND